D1523479

EXPLORE
MEXICO CITY

by Patricia Hutchison

STORY LIBRARY
MORE TO EXPLORE

www.12StoryLibrary.com

12-Story Library is an imprint of Bookstaves.

Photographs ©: Diego Grandi/Shutterstock.com, cover, 1; ChameleonsEye/Shutterstock.com, 4; aguinaldo matzenbacher/Shutterstock.com, 5; mehdi33300/Shutterstock.com, 6; PD, 7; Alex Cimbal/Shutterstock.com, 8; Kiev.Victor/Shutterstock.com, 9; NadyaRa/Shutterstock.com, 10; Thelmadatter/CC3.0, 11; Frontpage/Shutterstock.com, 12; Kamira/Shutterstock.com, 13; Robert_Hu/Shutterstock.com, 13; ChameleonsEye/Shutterstock.com, 14; Luis Alvarado Alvarado/Shutterstock.com, 14; Charles Harker/Shutterstock.com, 15; posztos/Shutterstock.com, 16; testing/Shutterstock.com, 17; Heide Pinkall/Shutterstock.com, 18; Santiago Castillo Chomel/Shutterstock.com, 19; Bill Perry/Shutterstock.com, 20; Aberu.Go/Shutterstock.com, 21; Inspired By Maps/Shutterstock.com, 22; Joshua Resnick/Shutterstock.com, 22; FrauTori/Shutterstock.com, 23; Elena Diego/Shutterstock.com, 23; Suriel Ramzal/Shutterstock.com, 24; Bentfotos/Shutterstock.com, 25; Aberu.Go/Shutterstock.com, 26; Gabriela ZZ/Shutterstock.com, 26; Byelikova Oksana/Shutterstock.com, 27; ChameleonsEye/Shutterstock.com, 28; seeyah panwan/Shutterstock.com, 29; Robert_Hu/Shutterstock.com, 30

ISBN
9781632357267 (hardcover)
9781632358356 (paperback)
9781645820130 (ebook)

Library of Congress Control Number: 2019938655

Printed in the United States of America
September 2019

About the Cover
Mexico City's Alameda Central Park and the Palace of Fine Arts.

Access free, up-to-date content on this topic plus a full digital version of this book. Scan the QR code on page 31 or use your school's login at 12StoryLibrary.com.

Table of Contents

A City Surrounded by Mountains

Popocatépetl is one of the most active volcanoes in Mexico.

Mexico City sits in the Valley of Mexico, high in a plateau at the center of the country. The elevation there is 7,349 feet (2,240 m). The ninth-largest city in the world covers about 573 square miles (1,485 sq km).

Geography affects Mexico City in many ways. Not all of them are good. Mexico Valley is part of the Trans-Mexican Volcanic Belt. Tall mountains and volcanoes surround the city. Water flows down to the valley. There is no natural outlet to drain the water. Parts of Mexico City often flood.

The city was built on an ancient lake bed. It stands on layers of sand and clay that lie deep below the buildings. During earthquakes, this unstable ground shakes like a bowl of gelatin. Homes and other buildings are damaged.

One advantage of Mexico City's geography is the climate. Its location causes pleasant weather most of the year. Winter temperatures

average around 70 degrees Fahrenheit (21°C). During summer, the highs are around 83 degrees Fahrenheit (28°C). From October through May, the air is dry. In the other months, Mexico City has rain almost every day. However, it rarely lasts more than an hour.

30

Number of feet (9.1 m) some buildings in Mexico City have sunk since 1900

- The water level of an aquifer under the city is dropping.
- As a result, the ground is sinking.
- What used to be the ground floor of the Palace of Fine Arts has become a basement.

MEXICO CITY SHAKES AND CRUMBLES

On September 19, 1985, an earthquake rocked Mexico City for two full minutes. Another one followed less than two days later. Ten thousand people lost their lives. Nearly 100,000 were left homeless. More than 1,000 buildings were destroyed. Most of the destruction happened near the center of the city.

Mexico City Has a Long History

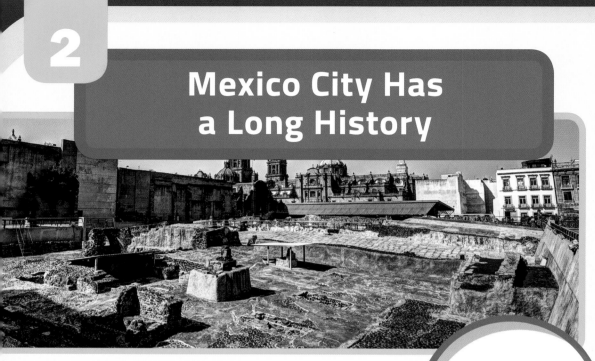

At the beginning of the 1300s, the Aztec people searched for a new home. Years later, they found it on an island in the middle of a lake. Their city was born in 1325. The people named it Tenochtitlán. Over the next 80 years, the territory grew, and the city became the center of a new empire.

Nearly 200 years later, Hernán Cortés visited the area. He wanted to claim the city for Spain. On August 13, 1521, he marched his forces into Tenochtitlán. The Spanish demolished the city. They built Mexico City on the ruins. It became one of the most important cities in the Americas.

Tenochtitlán's main temple was rediscoverd in the city in the early 20th century.

The Spanish ruled Mexico City for the next 300 years. In the early 1800s, Miguel Hidalgo y Costilla urged natives to fight for independence. The Catholic priest started an armed revolt in 1810. After a long and bloody battle, Mexico became an independent republic in 1823. The next year, the constitution was signed. A new government was created.

35

Number of years Porfirio Diaz stayed in power

- On November 29, 1876, Diaz appointed himself president.
- He assassinated his rivals to keep his hold on power.
- A revolution began in 1910, and Diaz stepped down the next year.

TIMELINE

1325: The city of Tenochtitlán is founded by the Aztecs.

1521: Tenochtitlán is destroyed by Spanish forces led by Cortés.

1824: The Mexican Federal District is created by the signing of the constitution.

1847: The Battle for Mexico City is fought as part of the Mexican-American War.

1848: The Treaty of Guadalupe Hidalgo is signed, ending the Mexican-American War.

1968: The Summer Olympics are held in Mexico City.

1995: The World Trade Center Mexico City opens.

2010: The population in the city is 8.851 million.

In 1846, Mexico City was invaded by the United States. The Mexican-American War ended with the signing of a treaty. Mexico was forced to give up a large part of its northern territory. During the War of Reform, Benito Juárez captured the city in 1867. In 1871, Porfirio Diaz overthrew the government and became dictator. These battles destroyed parts of Mexico City. But it stayed an important city. The population grew, and by 1950 three million people lived there. The city continued to improve throughout the next decades. Today Mexico City is a major economic and cultural center.

3

People from Other Countries Are Drawn to Mexico City

Almost nine million people live in the heart of Mexico City. More than 20 million live in the metropolitan area. Mexico City is a mixture of the old and new. People worship at a church built 300 years ago. Around the corner, they connect to Wi-Fi at a fast-food restaurant. Mexico City is the largest Spanish-speaking city in the world. But English is spoken in professional circles.

Over 90 percent of people in Mexico City can read and write. This is the highest percentage in the country. Students must attend nine years of school. Mexico City has some of the nation's most important universities and colleges.

Mexico City is the richest city in the country. However, the wealth is uneven. Almost 15 percent of

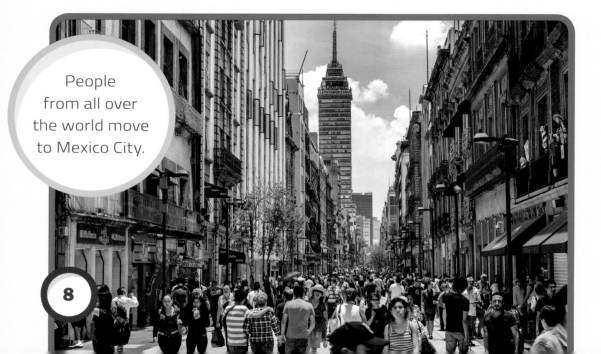

People from all over the world move to Mexico City.

8

The National Autonomous University of Mexico is a UNESCO World Heritage Site.

the city's people live in poverty. There are over 14,000 children living and working on the streets of Mexico City. They live in markets, bus stations, and city parks. This problem is growing, but the government is working on solving it.

People from all over the world migrate to Mexico City. Many indigenous peoples live there. Over 40 indigenous languages are spoken in the city. Large numbers of immigrants from Canada, the United States, South America, and Europe flock to Mexico City each year.

325,000
Number of students enrolled in the National Autonomous University of Mexico (UNAM)

- The university was founded in 1551.
- The campus includes an Olympic stadium.
- Covering 3.86 square miles (10 sq km), the campus is like a small city.

THINK ABOUT IT

People from all over the world move to Mexico City to live. What do you think attracts people to this city?

4

Mexico City Is an Important Economic Center

The financial sector is growing in the city.

Mexico City is the capital and economic support of the nation of Mexico. It generates revenue from various sources. The main industries produce iron and steel. Textiles, yarn, plastics, and furniture are also manufactured in the city.

Manufacturing is important, but it has been slowly pushed out of the capital. A service economy has taken its place. Tourism brings millions of dollars into the city. Visitors are attracted by the restaurants, hotels, and entertainment centers. These services employ millions of people.

Many large corporations have located their headquarters in Mexico City. Arca Continental bottles and distributes Coca-Cola products throughout the Western Hemisphere. Bimbo is the largest Mexican-owned baking company. It has branches in the Americas, Asia, and Europe. The city is becoming one of the world's financial capitals. It is home to

THINK ABOUT IT

The informal economy is popular in Mexico City. How might it both help and hurt the economy of the city?

1

Percent of Mexico City's economy that comes from manufacturing

- Factories have been moved to neighboring cities.
- The economies of those cities have been boosted.
- Pollution has been reduced in Mexico City.

large banking corporations such as Citigroup.

Mexico City also has an informal economy. Each day, thousands of vendors line the streets. They sell everything from food to umbrellas. If they didn't have their own businesses, these people would be unemployed. But they are a challenge to the city. For years, the government has tried to clear the vendors off the streets. They don't pay taxes or rent. Also, they often sell their products at discounted prices. Business owners complain because of the unfair competition.

Despite government efforts, vendors are on many streets.

Architecture Is a Mix of Old and New

Few buildings in Mexico City can be described as plain. The cityscape is a mixture of vivid colors and textures. Windows are often mismatched. Many buildings have bold paintings and colorful tile patterns. The architecture has changed as the city has grown. Ancient, classic, and modern styles blend together throughout the streets.

In the 1500s, the Spanish rebuilt Mexico City as a colony. Their architecture was based on the styles in Europe. The city's National

14

Number of courtyards in the National Palace

- The building takes up the entire east side of Mexico City's main square.
- Builders used stones from an ancient Aztec residence to build the palace.
- Today it houses government offices.

The National Palace was built in the Spanish Colonial style.

Palace is an example of this influence. The massive building includes domes, pointed arches, and ornate decorations. These are all elements from the Spanish Colonial style.

As Mexico began to work for independence, a new style of architecture became popular. Known as Mexican Baroque, it added lively decorations to the buildings. The Metropolitan Cathedral in Mexico City is an example of this style. The outside walls are covered in moldings of angels and saints. Inside, the tall, arched altar is covered with gold.

Modern architecture in the capital adds high-tech styles as well as folk art. An example is the Soumaya Museum. Built in 1994, the building has sweeping upward curves. The outside is covered with metallic plates. It looks like snakeskin shimmering in the sun.

CASTILLO CHAPULTEPEC MAKES ITS FILM DEBUT

Chapultepec Castle sits high on a hill in one of Mexico City's parks. It was once the home of Emperor Maximilian I and his wife, Charlotte. Today it is the National Museum of History. In 1996, the castle was used to film *Romeo and Juliet* starring Leonardo DiCaprio.

13

Infrastructure Tries to Keep Up with Growth

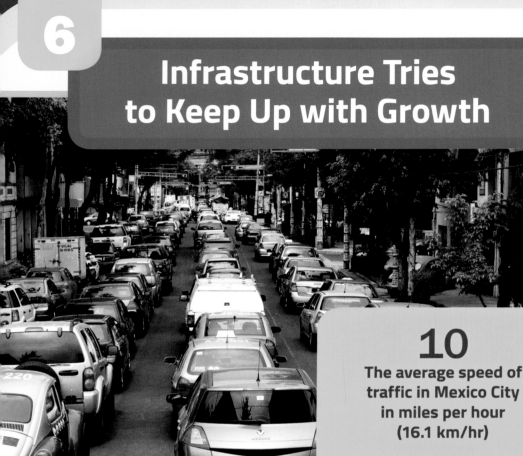

10

The average speed of traffic in Mexico City in miles per hour (16.1 km/hr)

- Traffic jams cost the economy $2.5 billion each year.
- The huge number of vehicles causes poor air quality in the city.
- To help with the problem, the city has started a bike sharing service.

In the capital, a knot of cars and trucks can appear instantly. It clogs the streets, forcing travelers to sit for hours. Mexico City is trying to find solutions to this traffic problem. But the government is having a tough time keeping up with the city's growth.

Only one-fourth of the people use their own cars. Others board bright red buses that

14

are supported by the government. Another choice are the *peseros*, Mexico City's minibuses. But these vehicles can get caught in traffic jams, too. Millions of commuters use the subway system. This is quicker than travelling on the streets and highways.

Housing is another challenge for Mexico City's infrastructure. To keep up with the growing population, at least 40,000 housing units need to be built each year. Only half of these are actually completed. As a result, shanties have popped up all over the city. More than half of the city's architecture is built without regulations. These buildings can be dangerous and unhealthy.

Mexico City is built on a lake bed. Still, getting clean water is a problem. The city's drainage system is old. Heavy rainfall causes flooding and mudslides. Sewage is often mixed with the drain water. Many residents have to buy their water from water trucks.

THINK ABOUT IT

Mexico City is building 500 housing units on 2.5 acres (1 hectare). An American suburb has about 12 units in the same size area. Would you like living as close together as people do in Mexico City?

15

Mexico City Has a Wealth of Culture

Mexico City is bursting with museums. The city's National Museum of Anthropology is the largest in Mexico. Visitors can see ancient tools, such as the Stone of the Sun, which the Aztecs used as a calendar. Other artifacts are on display at Temple Mayor. The temple was once the religious center for the Aztecs. It was uncovered in 1978. It is still an active archaeological site.

Children love the Papalote Museo del Niño. The museum has many hands-on activities. Kids can use their senses to solve problems and create art. People of all ages enjoy the Mucho Mundo Chocolate Museum. Here they learn the history, production, and effects of chocolate. There is even a room built with chocolate walls.

Mexico City has many fine auditoriums. The National Auditorium hosts music, theater, and opera. Book fairs and

The National Museum of Anthropology has many ancient artifacts that date back to the Aztecs.

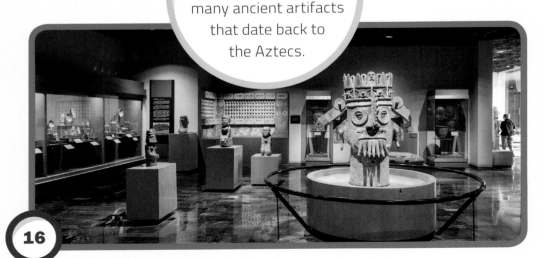

The Palace of Fine Arts is home to the Ballet Folklorico de Mexico.

photography exhibits are held on the large outdoor patio. As many as 10,000 people visit the Palace of Fine Arts each week. The auditorium there is home to the Ballet Folklorico de Mexico. Fans enjoy watching performers dance to folk music wearing colorful costumes.

HIGH-TECH AUDIO IN MEXICO CITY

Teatro Telcel, a performing arts theater, is located six floors underground. It has an advanced audio system. There are over 270 loudspeakers throughout the room. From each seat, the audience hears as if they were only about 20 feet (6 m) from the stage.

66,000
Works of art in the Soumaya Museum

- They were donated by Carlos Slim.
- Slim was once the richest man in the world.
- Many of the works are by famous artists including Monet and Picasso.

Mexico City Loves Sports

There is a sport for every type of fan in Mexico City. The sport they love most is football. Americans call it soccer. The Estadio Azteca stadium is the home of the Mexican National Football Team. Two World Cup finals were held there in 1970 and 1986. Famous players such as Antonio Carbajal and Hugo Sánchez have played at the stadium.

Fans love their Mexican National Football Team.

Sports from the United States have also become favorites in Mexico City. There is a professional basketball team. Ice hockey is also played in the city. A NASCAR race is held every year at the Autodrómo Hermanos Rodríguez. Fans gather at the Palacio de los Deportes to watch motocross competitions.

There are also plenty of sports in which to participate. Despite the mild climate, there is ice skating in the

The Mexico City Marathon has been held every year since 1983.

winter. The city has many golf courses, although most of them are private. Tennis courts attract players of all abilities. Horseback riding is offered in some of the city's public parks.

STREET SOCCER IN MEXICO CITY

Each year, homeless and at-risk youth are chosen from all over the world to play in the Homeless World Cup. To take part, they must show teamwork and leadership qualities. The games offer these youth a chance to make their lives better. Hundreds of thousands of fans watch every year. Mexico City hosted the games in 2012.

1968
Year when Mexico City hosted the Summer Olympics

- It was the first Latin American city to host the Games.
- The Olympic Stadium was built on the grounds of the National Autonomous University of Mexico.
- Mexican hurdler Enriqueta Basilio was the first woman ever to light the Olympic Cauldron at the Opening Ceremony.

Attractions Keep Visitors Busy

At the heart of Mexico City is the Zócalo. It is one of the largest public squares in the world. Since the days of the Aztecs, it has been an important place for public celebrations. It is officially known as Plaza de la Constitución. A giant Mexican flag stands at its center. The square also hosts religious ceremonies several times a year.

Several historic buildings border the Zócalo. The National Palace holds the executive branch of the Mexican government. Murals by Diego Rivera are painted across the palace walls. They show Mexican history from ancient times to the present. Along another side, the towers of the Metropolitan Cathedral cast shadows into

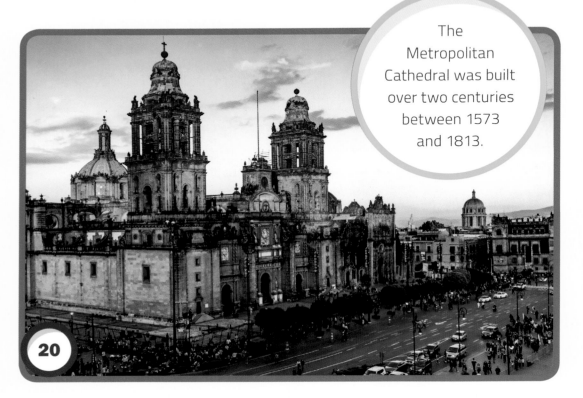

The Metropolitan Cathedral was built over two centuries between 1573 and 1813.

The Monumento a la Revolución commemorates the Mexican Revolution victory in 1920.

the square. It is the oldest cathedral in Latin America. It is made of stone from an ancient pyramid.

Paseo de la Reforma is a famous avenue in Mexico City. The Monumento a la Revolución sits along this street. The towering arch is one of the largest in the world. Pancho Villa and other heroes of the Mexican Revolution are buried there. The Revolutionary Museum at its base hosts exhibitions and events. One popular event is the annual Zombie Walk on the Day of the Dead.

Chapultepec Park in Mexico City is nearly twice the size of New York's Central Park. Long ago it was a retreat for Aztec rulers. Today it has a zoo and several museums. Hiking trails lined with trees wind around the lakes. Millions of people visit the park each year.

1529
Year when Alameda Central Park in Mexico City was built

- The park was originally an Aztec marketplace.
- Today cafés and shops sit along one edge.
- Fields of lavender fill the air with a wonderful scent.

Eating and Shopping in Mexico City

The best tacos *al pastor* are made by street vendors.

People in Mexico City love to eat. There are hundreds of fine restaurants. But street food is also very popular. Vendors along the streets prepare tacos *al pastor*, shaving meat and pineapple into tortillas. *Tlacoyos* are oval-shaped corn cakes stuffed with cheese and beans. *Barbacoa* is made by wrapping lamb in agave leaves. It is roasted in an underground pit. Tacos and tamales are also on the menu.

Bakers sell sweet breads all over the city. The most loved is the *concha*, shaped like a shell. This sweet roll is covered with a cookie crust. Sometimes they are split and filled with cream or custard.

Shoppers in Mexico City have many choices. There are modern malls as well as large street markets. Handmade items are popular. Glassblowing is an old art form. Crafters shape pitchers, bowls, and vases of brightly colored glass. Jewelers make rings and necklaces from silver set with turquoise stones.

Visitors and locals buy textiles such as blouses and shawls. Hand-embroidered huipils are wildly popular. Women have worn this

WANT SOME CHINICUILES WITH THAT?

They taste like crunchy French fries, but they are really red caterpillars. These pesky critters attack the agave plant. So eating them is helpful for the environment. Other treats found in Mexico City include fried escamoles (ant larvae) and toasted grasshoppers.

350
Number of local artists at the Garden of Art in Mexico City

- This is one of the largest outdoor art markets in the world.
- Shoppers can buy paintings, sculptures, and photography.
- Prices range from $5 to $500.

traditional one-piece garment since ancient times. Local artisans make napkins and tablecloths from cotton or linen. Shoppers also buy pottery and Mexican chocolate flavored with chilies.

11

Daily Life Moves at a Slow Pace

Traffic is a huge problem in Mexico City. Workers often spend two hours getting to their jobs. They work eight hours. Then they spend another two hours getting home. Eating a relaxing lunch is one of the pleasures of life in the city. *La comida* (lunch) is served from 2 p.m. to 4 p.m. It is the largest meal of the day. A lighter meal of tamales or tacos is served around 10 p.m.

The cost of living in the capital is low. Public transportation is less than one dollar. Food is also inexpensive. Even at restaurants, most dishes are less than 20 dollars.

Mexico City is noisy. Cars zoom by, honking their horns. Dogs bark, church bells ring, and people shout. On the weekends, some streets are shut down. Lively parties with loud music go on late into the night.

Most schools in Mexico City offer preschool classes. This education

People enjoy getting together in their neighborhoods.

starts at age three. School classes run from 8 a.m. to 3 p.m. Children in primary school learn English, Spanish, math, geography, and science. Textbooks are free at this level. Students in grades 7 through 12 must pay for their books.

Mexico City is made up of hundreds of small neighborhoods. Richer parts of town are surrounded by slums. Poverty is everywhere. Millions of people live in houses made of cardboard. Homeless children beg for money in trendy bars and cafés.

12
Number of square feet (1.1 sq m) in a typical shanty house

- Shanties are built right alongside more expensive homes.
- They usually have two rooms.
- Seven or more family members sleep in one room.

Mexico City Has Much to Celebrate

Festivals and celebrations light up Mexico City all year. One of the most important is the Festival del Centro Histórico. It is the largest cultural event in the country. Every spring, it takes place in the Zócalo, the city's historic center. For two weeks every March, there are all kinds of performances including dances, music, operas, and plays.

September 16 is Mexico's Independence Day. It honors Mexico's constitution. The celebration begins at 11 p.m. on September 15. The president of Mexico comes to the balcony of the National Palace and shouts, "Viva México!" The crowd shouts back, "Viva!" The next day, there is lively music and dancing at the city's historic centers.

Rosca de reyes cake is served on Three Kings' Day.

9

Number of days Mexicans celebrate Las Posadas

- The celebration takes place from December 16 to 24.
- Children parade around the houses, dressed as shepherds and angels.
- Afterwards there are music, firecrackers, and piñatas.

HONORING THE DEAD

On November 1, Mexicans celebrate Dia de los Muertos (Day of the Dead). This is a day to remember loved ones who have died. Mexico City has its own festival on that day. A city park hosts a celebration with tamales and other traditional foods. Homes are decorated with *calaveras*, miniature skulls painted with bright colors.

Religious celebrations fill the calendar. In January, the city celebrates Epiphany. This holiday is called Three Kings' Day. People serve a cake called the *rosca de reyes*, or ring of the kings. It has a little doll hidden inside that symbolizes the baby Jesus. The guest who gets the doll in his or her slice of cake must host the next celebration. Catholics from all over the world arrive at the Basilica of Our Lady of Guadalupe on December 12. This feast day honors the patron saint of Mexico City and the Americas.

People dress in costume for the annual Day of the Dead parade in Mexico City.

Fun Facts about Mexico City

- Area: 573 square miles (1,485 sq km).
  Population in 2019: 8.9 million.

- More than 600,000 Americans live in Mexico City. This is the largest concentration of Americans living outside of the USA.

- Mexico City set the world record in 2010 for the biggest enchilada ever made. It was 230 feet long (70 m) and weighed almost 1.5 tons (1,361 kg).

- The tower on the city's General Dr. Manuel Gea González Hospital has special tiles that break down pollution in the air. Each day, the tiles reduce pollution equal to 1,000 cars.

- Every winter, the city's famous Zócalo turns into one of the world's biggest ice-skating rinks.

- This was the first city to host an NFL regular season game outside of the United States. The game took place in 2005 at the Estadio Azteca stadium. The Arizona Cardinals defeated the San Francisco 49ers by a score of 31 to 14.

- Mexico is in the Ring of Fire, one of the earth's most violent earthquake and volcano zones.

- Mexico City has the biggest bullring in the world. It can hold 41,000 people.

Where in the World?

Mexico City

Glossary

aquifer
A layer of spongy rock that can hold or move groundwater.

artifacts
Ancient objects made by humans.

cityscape
The landscape or appearance of a city.

commuters
People who travel some distance to work every day.

financial
Having to do with money.

indigenous
People who are native to a certain place.

informal
Not officially approved.

infrastructure
The basic organizational and physical structures needed to operate a city, such as roads, buildings, power supplies, and communication systems.

metropolitan
The area surrounding a large city.

republic
A state in which power is held by the people and their elected government.

revenue
Income or earnings from business.

Read More

Brooks, Susie. *Unpacked: Mexico*. London, UK: Hachette Children's Group, 2016.

Carswell, Heather, et al. *The Cities Book: A Journey through 86 of the World's Greatest Cities*. Victoria, Australia: Lonely Planet Kids, 2016.

Markovics, Joyce L. *Mexico City.* New York: Bearport Publishing, 2018.

Murray, Lily. *A World of Cities*. Somerville, MA: Candlewick Studio, 2018.

Visit 12StoryLibrary.com

Scan the code or use your school's login at **12StoryLibrary.com** for recent updates about this topic and a full digital version of this book. Enjoy free access to:

- Digital ebook
- Breaking news updates
- Live content feeds
- Videos, interactive maps, and graphics
- Additional web resources

Note to educators: Visit 12StoryLibrary.com/register to sign up for free premium website access. Enjoy live content plus a full digital version of every 12-Story Library book you own for every student at your school.

Index

About the Author

Patricia Hutchison is a former teacher.
She has written dozens of nonfiction
children's books about science,
nature, history, and geography.
She lives in South Carolina with
her husband. They love to travel
throughout the United States and to
other countries.

READ MORE FROM 12-STORY LIBRARY

Every 12-Story Library Book
is available in many fomats.
For more information, visit
12StoryLibrary.com

32